Basics

half-hitch knot

Come out a bead and form a loop perpendicular to the thread between beads. Bring the needle under the thread away from the loop. Then go back over the thread and through the loop. Pull gently so the knot doesn't tighten prematurely.

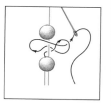

square knot

1 Bring the left-hand cord over the right-hand cord and around.
2 Cross right over left and go through the loop.

surgeon's knot

An extra wrap makes the top curl around the sides for a stronger knot. Begin as a square knot: left over right and around, then right over left and through (figures 1 and 2, above). Go through the loop again, then tighten.

crimping

1 Position the crimp bead in the notch closest to the crimping pliers' handle.
2 Separate the wires and firmly squeeze the crimp.

3 Move the crimp into the notch at the pliers' tip and hold the crimp as shown. Squeeze the crimp bead, folding it in half at the indentation.

4 Tug the clasp to make sure the folded crimp is secure.

loops: plain

1 Trim the wire ⅜ in. (1cm) above the top bead. Make a right angle bend close to the bead.
2 Grab the wire's tip with roundnose pliers. Roll the wire to form a half circle. Release the wire.

3 Reposition the pliers in the loop and continue rolling.
4 The finished loop should form a centered circle above the bead.

loops: wrapped

1 Make sure you have no less than 1¼ in. (32mm) of wire above your bead. With the tip of your chainnose pliers, grasp the wire directly above the bead. Bend the wire (above the pliers) into a right angle.
2 Using roundnose pliers, position the jaws vertically in the bend.

3 Bring the wire over the top jaw of the roundnose pliers.
4 Keep the jaws vertical and reposition the pliers so the lower jaw fits snugly in the loop. Curve the wire downward around the bottom of the roundnose pliers. This is the first half of a wrapped loop. At this point, string on chain or other elements as needed.

5 Position the jaws of your chainnose pliers across the loop.
6 Wrap the wire around the wire stem, covering the stem between the loop and the bead. Trim the excess wire and gently press the cut end close to the wraps with chainnose pliers.

rings: opening and closing

1 Hold the jump ring with two pairs of chainnose pliers or chainnose and roundnose pliers, as shown.

2 To open the jump ring, bring one pair of pliers toward you and push the other away.
3 Reverse the steps to close the open jump ring.

Duo-tone spiral rope set

As simple as it is versatile, spiral rope is a favorite stitch for many beaders. This variation on a basic design was inspired by the contrast between the smooth, regular shapes of freshwater pearls and the rough, irregular shapes of gemstone chips. Using two different colors accentuates the contrast.

To create your own duo-tone jewelry set, begin by choosing two colors of gemstones in dramatic contrast such as amethyst and peridot, or smoky quartz and citrine. Then choose two colors of freshwater pearls and a mix of seed beads that coordinate with the chips. Designate these colors "A" and "B" as you see fit.

getting started

This choker is designed to be 15½ in. (39cm) long. Make the first 6½ in. (16.5cm) of the necklace in color A. To allow the ends of the necklace to taper toward the clasp, the first five spirals do not contain gemstone chips or pearls. For a different overall measurement, adjust the lengths of the color segments accordingly.

❶ Thread a #10 needle with about 15 in. (38cm) of Power Pro. This strong braided thread makes a much stronger clasp attachment than regular beading threads.

❷ String six size 14º seed beads and then the loop of one side of the clasp, leaving a 6-in. (15cm) tail. Pass back through all six beads again so that a snug loop of beads is formed around the clasp loop. Tie a square knot (see "Basics," p. 3). Do not cut the tail.

❸ In a bowl, mix small quantities of the various size 11º color A seed beads until you have a pleasing mixture. In a separate bowl, do the same for the size 11º color B seed beads.

choker

Spiral rope consists of an inner core of beads with an outer spiral made of repeating half circles or arcs. For this necklace, size 8º beads form the inner core, and size 11º beads and pearls or gem chips form the outer spiral. Since gemstone chips can vary greatly in size, you will need to experiment a bit to find the right number of chips to use in the spirals to get the fullness that appeals to you.

❶ String four size 8º beads in color A for the core, then string the following for the spiral: three size 11º, one size 8º, and three size 11º in color A.

❷ To form the first loop, pass back through all four core beads in the same direction. Pull snug. With the clasp hanging down, hold the arc with your nondominant hand. If you are right-handed, you will be holding the arc in your left hand and the arc is shaped like a C. If you are left-handed, the arc is shaped like a backward C (**figure 1**). As you continue working spiral rope, always keep the arcs facing in this same direction.

3 To form the next loop, string one 8º core bead, three 11ºs, one 8º, and three 11ºs in color A. Pass back through the last three core beads strung in step 1 and the single core bead strung in this step (**figure 2**). In all succeeding loops, you will always pass back through the last three core beads strung in the previous loops plus the new core bead strung in the current loop. Each newly formed arc lies on top of the one made before it. The top of each newly formed arc is always one bead higher than the one made before it.

4 Repeat step 3 three more times for a total of five loops made only with seed beads. End this thread with two half-hitch knots (see "Basics"). Leave the tail for now.

5 Thread a #12 needle (a smaller needle is usually necessary with gemstones and pearls; if the holes in your pearls and gemstones are sufficiently large, feel free to continue using the #10 needle) with conditioned Nymo or C-Lon thread. Tie on a stop bead. Enter the core five or six beads beneath the one where you left off with the needle pointing up toward the unfinished work; pass through a few beads and tie the working thread to a base thread with two half-hitch knots. Pass through the remaining core beads until you exit at the same point you left the previous thread's tail. Tie the new thread and the Power Pro tail together with a square knot. After working with the new thread a while, weave both tails back through several core beads and clip them close to the work.

6 Beginning with the sixth loop, omit the size 8º bead in the middle of the spiral and include pearls or gemstone chips instead. The pattern for the outer loops will vary, depending on the size of your gemstone chips and how full you want your necklace to be. Each loop should consist of seven or

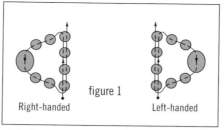

figure 1

Right-handed   Left-handed

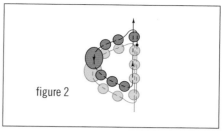

figure 2

eight beads each. This example shows one pearl spiral for every three or four gem chip spirals. Continue working with color A for 6½ in.

7 Gradually transition from color A to B in the front 2½ in. (6.4cm) of the choker. Start by adding one gem chip in color B in a spiral made up of mostly color A beads. In succeeding loops, gradually increase the number of color B beads, chips, and pearls, including the core beads, and decrease the number of color A beads, chips, and pearls.

8 For the last 6½ in., use beads, chips, and pearls in color B only.

9 When you are about 1½ in. (3.8cm) from the end, tie off your thread as you did in step 4. Thread a #10 needle with about 15 in. of Power Pro.

10 Work the last five loops with 8ºs for the core as usual and the following for the spiral as you did in step 1: three size 11º, one size 8º, three size 11º. Tie off as you did in step 4.

11 String six size 14º seed beads and the loop of the other side of the clasp, leaving a 6-in. tail. Pass back through all the beads again so that a snug loop of beads is formed around the clasp's loop. Go through several core beads and tie two half-hitch knots. Repeat a couple of times and trim the thread close to the work. Finish any remaining tails in the same manner.

earrings

1 Thread a #10 or 12 needle with about 2 ft. (61cm) of conditioned Nymo or C-Lon thread. String six size 14º beads and an earring wire loop, leaving a 6-in. tail. Go back through all six beads again so that a snug loop of beads is formed around the earring wire's loop. Tie a square knot. Do not cut the tail now.

2 Using the same stringing patterns you used in step 6 of the choker, work ten loops of spiral rope in color A. As before, you will use size 8º seed beads

consistently for the core, and the spirals will consist of size 11º seed beads and gem chips or pearls.

3 After forming the last loop, tie two half-hitch knots between the core bead where your thread exits and the adjacent 11º outer spiral bead. Pass back through the 11º. String one 11º, one pearl, and one 14º. Pass back through the pearl and the 11º and pull snug.

4 To secure, pass back through several core beads and tie two half-hitch knots. Pass back through the rest of the core beads until you reach the tail you left behind. Tie a square knot with the tail and working thread. Pass back through a few core beads and trim thread close to the work. Thread the needle with the tail and pass back through a few core beads; trim the tail close to the work.

5 Make the other earring to match in color B. ● – *Tina Koyama*

materials

- **2** 16-in. (41cm) strands of gemstone chips, **1** each of two contrasting colors (designate the colors A and B)
- **2** 16-in. strands of freshwater pearls, **1** each in colors that coordinate with gemstone chips A and B
- size 8º seed beads to match gemstone chips in both color A and color B
- size 11º seed beads in various shades to coordinate with both colors A and B
- **26** size 14º seed beads to coordinate with both colors A and B
- Beadsmith's Power Pro braided beading thread, .006
- Nymo D or C-Lon thread to coordinate with both colors A and B (or a neutral color)
- beeswax or Thread Heaven for Nymo
- clasp
- **2** earring wires
- beading needles, #10 and 12

Coiled bead bracelet

Wrapping a bead with a coil of wire lends it a dramatic touch, and the combinations you can play with are virtually endless. You can recreate the coiled Bali beads as shown above, coil silver over gold garlic beads as shown on p. 7, or work with semi-precious stones to add a splash of color. You may also opt to wear a bracelet's length of coiled beads as a necklace by attaching a chain to each clasp end.

❶ Cut an 18-in. (46cm) length of 16-gauge wire and straighten it out as much as possible.

❷ Fold the 22-gauge wire in half and place the fold against the cut piece of 16-gauge wire. Working one end at a time, wrap the 22-gauge wire in a tight coil around the 16-gauge core, keeping the wraps even and close together (**photo a**).

❸ Slide the coil off the 16-gauge wire. Cut the coil into four 3½-in. (9cm) segments and the core wire into four 4½-in. (11.4cm) segments. Slide each coil back onto a core wire (**photo b**).

❹ Cut four 1⅞ in. (4.8cm) pieces of 16-gauge wire (or approximately 1⅜ in./ 3.5cm longer than the beads). Turn

a plain loop, (see "Basics," p. 3) on one end of each piece.

❺ Before you attach the coils to the wires prepared in step 4, wrap each coil around a cylinder that's about the same diameter as your beads to help start the spiral (**photo c**).

❻ Wrap or pinch one end of the core wire around the straight wire close to the loop. String a bead onto the straight wire, wrap the coil around the bead, and connect the other end of the core to the straight wire with another tight wrap.

Finish the assembly by trimming the straight wire to about ½ in. (1.3cm).

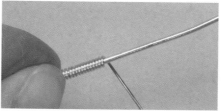

a

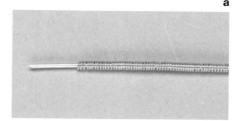

b

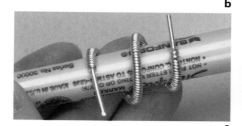

c

d

e

f

materials

- **7-8** 13mm Bali or other beads
- **40 in. (1m)** 16-gauge sterling silver wire, dead soft
- **11 ft. (3.4m)** 22-gauge sterling silver wire, dead soft
- **7mm** sterling silver soldered jump ring

Tools: roundnose and chainnose pliers, wire cutters, hammer, and anvil

Optional: Black Max or liver of sulfur, polishing cloth

Make another loop that's the same size and in the same plane as the first (**photo d**).

7 To prepare the plain bead components, cut four 1½-in. (3.8cm) pieces of 16-gauge wire (or about 1 in./2.5cm longer than the beads). Turn a plain loop at one end of each piece as in step 4, string a bead on each wire, and turn a plain loop on the other side. Keep the loops in the same plane and close to the bead (**photo e**).

8 To assemble the bracelet, open the loop on a plain bead, connect it to a coiled bead component, and close the loop (**photo f**). Alternate between coiled beads and plain beads until you reach the desired length (seven or eight components).

9 Using 16-gauge wire, make a clasp hook as shown in the **figure** above. Hammer it on both sides to flatten and harden it, then connect it to the loop at one end of the bracelet.

Attach a soldered jump ring to the loop on the other end of the bracelet to complete the clasp.

10 You can darken the silver by dipping the bracelet into an oxidizing chemical such as liver of sulfur or Black Max (if you have used gold beads, do not use an oxidizing agent). Then, polish the silver with a cloth, leaving the recesses of the coils dark and the raised surfaces gleaming. ● – *Wendy Witchner*

Fabulous findings

For an outstanding piece of jewelry, combine semi-precious gems and sterling silver, placing an emphasis on an unusual clasp or finding. Only the simplest stringing techniques are used but the result is elegant and sophisticated. Only you will know how easy it really was to make.

bracelet

❶ Determine the desired length of your bracelet (this one is 7 in./18cm), multiply that by five, and cut a piece of flexible beading wire to that length (here, 35 in./89cm).

❷ Wrap a piece of tape around one end of the wire to keep the beads from sliding off while you work. String a random mixture of beads and silver (**photo a**), stopping 3 in. (7.5cm) from the end.

❸ String a crimp bead, four or five beads, and a crimp bead.

❹ Remove the tape from the first end. Holding both wires tightly, pass the wire end that was taped through the crimp, the last beads strung, and the second crimp.

❺ Pull the ends of both wires so all the beads are snug and there are no gaps along the strand. With crimping pliers, crimp one crimp bead and then the other (see "Basics," p. 3 and **photo b**).

❻ Pass each wire through a few more beads if possible. Trim the excess wire.

❼ Grasp opposite ends of the completed loop, twist it two or three times, and fold it in half once (**photo c**). Slip the tip of the open clasp through the loops at one end of the strand (**photo d**). Put the bracelet around your wrist, catch the loops at the other end in the clasp, and close it.

necklace

❶ Cut a 5½-ft. (1.7m) length of flexible beading wire.

❷ To make the necklace, repeat steps 2-6 of "bracelet."

❸ To make the beaded dangle, turn a wrapped loop at one end of a 6-in. (15cm) piece of 18-gauge wire (see "Basics"). On the wire's other end, slide a 14mm bead, a 10-12mm flat silver spacer, a 12-14mm disk bead, and a 24mm bead (see the dangle at left).

❹ Make a tiny loop to secure the

materials

bracelet
• assortment of 2-6mm faceted stones or glass beads, crystals or pearls, sterling silver beads, and flat spacer beads
• flexible beading wire, .012-.014
• clasp/shortener (Pacific Silverworks, www.pacificsilverworks.com, 805-641-1394)
• **2** crimp beads

necklace
• assortment of 2-6mm faceted stones or glass beads, crystals or pearls, sterling silver beads, and flat spacer beads
• 6 in. (15cm) 18-gauge sterling silver wire
• 14mm focal bead
• 24mm focal bead
• 12-14mm disk-shaped bead
• 10-12mm flat spacer bead
• flexible beading wire, .012-.014
• clasp/shortener (Pacific Silverworks, www.pacificsilverworks.com, 805-641-1394)
• **2** crimp beads

Tools: roundnose and chainnose pliers, crimping pliers, wire cutters, tape

beads on the dangle (**photo e**). Slide the wrapped loop over the tongue on the clasp and let it hang from the component.

❺ One way to wear this necklace is to loop the strand over your head two or three times and use the clasp as a pendant (photo at left). To wear it as a choker, repeat the wrap from step 7 of "bracelet" and omit the dangle. ●
– Gillian Sampson

a

b

c

d

e

Beaded Goddess

Making beaded figures is a great way to get your creative juices flowing, especially when they incorporate wire into the design. Wire is so versatile and can be shaped into almost any form. Adding beads brings the form to life, creating depth and texture. Form the wire frame for the goddess, and then embellish her in sections.

❶ Use **photo a** as a guide to shape a 34-in. (86cm) length of 18-gauge wire into the goddess frame. Start by bending the wire in half and shaping it from the top of the head down on one side. Use 9½ in. (24cm) to go from the center top to **point d** on each side. Use the remainder to go from **point d** and complete the spiral.

❷ Cut four 4-in. (10cm) lengths of 24-gauge wire. Secure the goddess frame by wrapping one piece at **points a, b, c,** and **d** as shown in **photo a.** After several wraps, trim the wire close to the frame.

❸ Cut a 1-yd. (.9m) length of 24-gauge wire and secure the end by wrapping five times around the lower left side of the center section. Thread a 4-6mm accent bead and wrap the wire twice around the right side of the center section (**photo b**). String one or two accent beads and wrap twice around the left side of the center section. Repeat, crisscrossing up the center section, stringing as many accent beads as space permits.

❹ Halfway up the center section, string a 4mm or smaller bead, the alphabet beads to spell "fly" or some other three-letter word, and another 4mm or smaller bead (**photo c**). (Omit the edge beads if spelling a longer word.) String another three rows. Add the charm on the next row (**photo d**). Continue stringing and

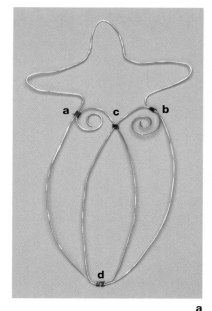

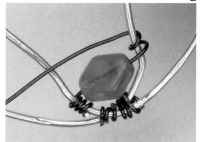

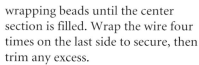

a

b

c

d

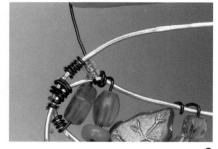

e

f

wrapping beads until the center section is filled. Wrap the wire four times on the last side to secure, then trim any excess.

❺ Cut a 1-yd. length of 24-gauge wire and wrap it five times around the bottom edge of the frame's bottom left section. String two color A seed beads and wrap once around the section's inside edge (**photo e**). Because this wire is already wrapped with the center section beads, you will have to wrap the new wire between the first set of wraps. Continue stringing rows of A beads to fill the space. Because you are wrapping only once around each wire edge, the rows will overlap, alternately sitting to the

front and then the back of the form (**photo f**).

❻ When ¼ in. (6mm) of the section remains before the spiral, switch to accent beads for the last two rows (**photo g, p. 12**). End the wire by wrapping five times around the frame and trim any excess.

g

h

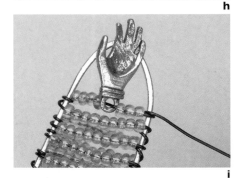

i

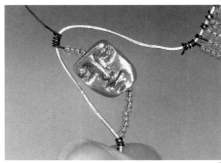

j

materials

- 34 in. (.86m) 18-gauge silver craft wire
- 7 yd. (6.4m) 24-gauge craft wire, colored to match bead choice
- **140-200** 4-10mm accent beads
- hank size 11º seed beads, color A
- ½ hank size 11º seed beads, color B
- **70-100** size 8º seed beads
- cube-shaped alphabet beads to spell "FLY" (or another three- or four-letter word)
- **1** face bead, **1** left and **1** right hand charm (available at www.primitiveearthbeads.com or Bead Source, 818-708-0972)
- decorative charm (dragonfly, flower, animal, etc.)

Tools: roundnose and chainnose pliers, diagonal wire cutters

❾ String four A beads, the right hand charm, and four A beads and wrap on the opposite edge (**photo i**). Space about five wraps around the frame until you reach the fingers. Bring the wire across the fingers and wrap along the other side to match. Trim the excess wire.

❿ Repeat steps 8 and 9 to complete the left arm.

⓫ Cut a 24-in. (61cm) length of 24-gauge wire and wrap the end five times around the bend between the left arm and the head. String ten A beads, the face bead, and four A beads. Wrap six times around the top center of the frame's head (**photo j**). Pick up four A beads, pass back through the face bead, and string ten A beads. Wrap three times around the bend between the head and right arm. Do not trim the wire.

⓬ Pick up five or six 8º seed beads, a leaf bead, and five or six 8º beads. Form a loop and wrap three times about ¼ in. up the frame from the last wrap (**photo k**). Repeat four times to make five hair loops around the frame's head. Wrap the wire five times to secure it and trim the excess.

⓭ Cut an 18-in. length of 24-gauge wire and secure it to the bend between the frame's head and left arm. String accent beads and wrap at the bend between the right arm and lower body (**photo l**). String more accent beads and wrap at the bend between the left arm and lower body. Wrap two more rows of accent beads to fill in across the upper

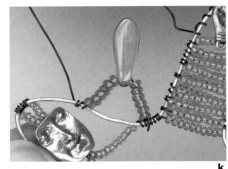

k

l

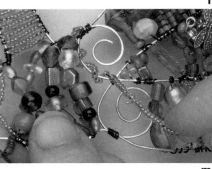

m

body. Wrap diagonally to the bend between the right arm and lower body, string accent beads, and wrap at the bend between the head and the left arm. Secure with a few more wraps and trim the excess.

⓮ Cut a 15-in. (38cm) length of 24-gauge wire and wrap four or five times at the connection of the right spiral to the frame. String 3 in. (7.6cm) of A beads on the wire and wrap the beaded wire in a loose coil around the top of the spiral to the intersection with the left spiral (**photo m**). Then wrap loosely round the top of the left spiral to the frame. Remove excess beads and wrap four to five times to end the wire. Trim any wire tails. ❍ *– Ronda Kivett*

❼ Repeat step 5 to fill the bottom right section with color B seed beads. End with two accent bead rows as you did in step 6.

❽ Cut an 18-in. (46cm) length of 24-gauge wire. Wrap the wire end five times at the bend between the head and right arm. String 10-12 A beads across the width of the right arm and wrap (**photo h**). Add rows of A beads to fill the arm, stopping ½ in. (1.3cm) from the end of the section.

Dangling flower necklace

Make a pretty, delicate necklace with a few vintage flower beads dangled from jump rings. This design has a Victorian feel, reflecting those days long past when gardens filled with flowers were surely abundant and the blossoms picked for a bouquet spoke a language of their own.

First make five flower dangles and 17 crystal links (**photo a**). Then link all the parts together and attach the clasp.

❶ To make a flower dangle, string a crystal, a flower, a silver bead, and a crystal on a head pin. Make a small loop above the last crystal (see "Basics," p. 3). Repeat four more times for five dangles.
❷ Open the loop on a dangle ("Basics") and string a soldered jump ring. Close the loop. Repeat with the other dangles.
❸ To make a link, make a small loop on an end of 1 in. (2.5cm) of wire. String a crystal and make another loop in the same plane as the first. Repeat 16 more times.
❹ Cut the chain in half. Open the loop on one end of a crystal link and attach it

a

b

c

materials

- **5** vintage flower beads (Eclectica, www.eclecticabeads.com, 262-641-0910)
- **27** 4mm fire-polished crystals
- **5** 3mm silver beads
- **11** 5-6mm silver soldered jump rings
- **2** 5mm silver jump rings
- **5** silver headpins
- **20** in. (51cm) 20-gauge silver wire, half-hard
- **14**-in. length (36cm) silver crinkle chain
- clasp

Tools: chainnose and roundnose pliers, diagonal wire cutters

to an end of one piece of chain. Close. *Add a soldered jump ring to the loop on the other end of the crystal and then a crystal link to the soldered jump ring (**photo b**). Repeat from * five more

times. Attach the last link added to an end of the second piece of chain.
❺ Attach one crystal link to the first and the last soldered jump rings in the necklace and two crystal links to each of the four middle jump rings.
❻ Starting at one end, attach two crystal links to a dangle (**photo c**). Repeat until all the dangles are added.
❼ Add a jump ring and then half the clasp to each chain end. ● – *Irina Miech*

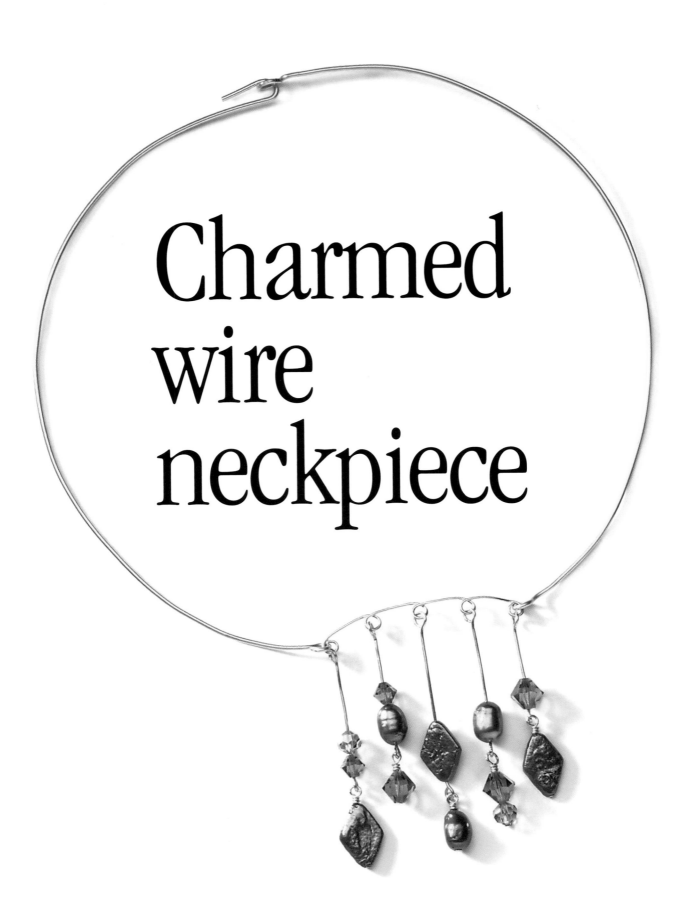

Charmed wire neckpiece

This elegant neckwire with five beaded dangles will take you less than two hours to make. Actually, you'll probably spend longer choosing the beads than you'll spend making the necklace! Make loops on a short piece of wire for the centerpiece. Then link side wires to the centerpiece and hang dangles from each of the loops.

❶ Cut a 5-in. (12.5cm) length of 20-gauge wire and make a loop (see "Basics," p. 3) on the last ⅜ in. (1cm).

❷ Place the loop against the tape measure and mark the wire ½ in. (1.3cm) past it.

❸ Grasp the wire on the loop side of the mark with roundnose pliers and pull the wire around the pliers until you can't pull it any further without distorting it (**photo a**). Rotate the pliers in the loop so you can pull the length of wire over the top of the jaw into a straight line with the wire between the two loops (**photo b**). Repeat twice more.

❹ Mark the wire ⅞ in. (2.2cm) past the fourth loop and cut off the excess. Make a loop with the last ⅜ in. All five loops point in the same direction.

❺ Cut one 9-in. (23cm) and one 10-in. (25cm) piece of 16-gauge wire and make a loop with the last ⅜ in. on one end of each.

❻ Open the loops (see "Basics")on the ends of the centerpiece and attach one of the heavier wire loops to each. These loops must meet at a right angle. Close the loops.

❼ Shape the side wires into the desired neckwire curve. Holding the piece up to your neck, cut the shorter wire off ½ in. past the center back of your neck. Make a large loop in the same plane as the loop that attaches it to the center.

❽ Try the necklace for fit and grasp the longer wire at the spot where you

a

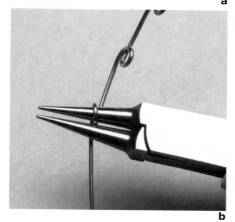

b

c

d

want it to hook into the back loop.

❾ Use roundnose pliers to bend the end of the wire into a hook shape (**photo c**). Trim off the excess length on the hook and file the end smooth.

❿ String one or more beads a head pin. Make a wrapped loop (see "Basics") at the top. Repeat four times to make five dangles.

⓫ Cut five pieces of 20-gauge wire to varying lengths. Make a loop on one end of a piece of wire, string one or more beads, and make another loop at the top. Open the bottom loop and attach a head pin unit. Repeat four times to complete the dangles (**photo d**).

⓬ Hook the top loop of each dangle to one of the loops on the centerpiece. ◗
– Louise Malcolm

materials
- **10** or more beads for dangles
- **5** head pins
- **5-18 in.** (12.5-46cm) 20-gauge wire, half hard
- **20 in.** (51cm) 16-gauge wire, half-hard

Tools: roundnose and chainnose pliers, diagonal wire cutters, marking pen, tape measure, small metal file

Using the simplest techniques, turn tantalizing pearl clusters into gorgeous jewelry that goes with the most elegant attire. Try using crystals or fire-polished glass if you want sparkle instead of luster, or go fun and funky with glass or metal beads. You can achieve whatever style you want with this versatile design.

pearl cluster

Make the pendant from 19 components that you attach to a piece of chain.

❶ Start with a head pin and string a daisy spacer, a 7-7.5mm pearl (wide end first) and a 6mm bead cap.

❷ With diagonal wire cutters, trim the head pin ⅜ in. (1cm) above the cap.

❸ Make a simple loop (see "Basics," p. 3) above the cap. This completes one component (**photo a**). Make 18 more.

❹ Open a component's loop (see "Basics") and attach it to the bottom link on a 1½ in. (4cm) length of chain. Close the loop. Attach two or three more components to this link.

❺ Experiment with the placement of the remaining pearls before you close the loops. As you work up the chain, skip a link if needed. Hang all the components, then adjust their placement until you are happy with the fullness and drape of the cluster. When satisfied, close the loops.

❻ Trim any excess links from the chain with wire cutters.

bail

To attach the pearl cluster to the neck cord, you can purchase a bail or make one. If you purchase one, attach it to the cluster and go on to "clasp," p. 17.

❶ Wrap 4 in. (10cm) of 22-gauge twisted wire around a size 8 (5mm) knitting needle.

❷ With diagonal wire cutters, trim the piece to four wraps (**photo b**). File the ends with a small file.

❸ Grasp the center of a 4-in. piece of 22-gauge round wire with chainnose pliers at a point where the jaw is less than 3/16 in. (5mm) wide. Bend both ends at a 90-degree angle (**photo c**).

❹ Remove the wire, grasp one side with the tip of the chainnose pliers and bend it at a 90-degree angle (**photo d**).

Clusters of pearls

5 Grasp the wire again and make a 90-degree angle (**photo e**).

6 Repeat steps 4-5 with the other side of the wire, to create a T-shaped piece.

7 Slip the coil from step 2 into this piece (**photo f**).

8 Wrap one leg of the T around the other (**photo g**). Trim the excess wire.

9 Trim the straight wire to ⅜ in. above the wrap and form a loop (**photo h**). Open the loop and attach the bail to the top link on the pendant. Close the loop.

clasp

1 Cut a 6-in. (15cm) piece of 24-gauge twisted wire. Wrap one end around a size 3 (3.25mm) knitting needle. Make seven or eight wraps.

2 Trim the excess to ⅜ in. above the last wrap. Grasp the tip of the wire with roundnose pliers and make a loop (**photo i**).

3 Repeat step 1.

4 Trim the excess to 1 in. (2.5cm) and bend it in half. With roundnose pliers, grasp the tip of the wire and form a hook by rolling the pliers inward. **Photo j** shows the completed clasp parts.

finishing

1 Dip the ends of the satin cord in glue and let them dry. Slide the pearl cluster onto the neck cord.

2 Use a twisting motion to slide one clasp piece onto each end of the cord. With chainnose pliers, gently compress the clasp around the cord.

a

b

Don't smash it. Apply a drop of glue to the cord through the top opening in each clasp end.

make the earrings

1 Follow steps 1-3 of "Pearl cluster" with these changes: slide a 15° seed, a

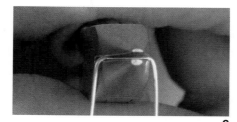

c

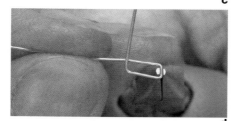

d

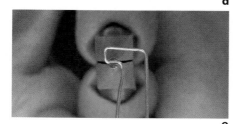

e

f

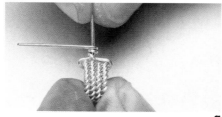

g

h

3-4mm pearl, and a 4mm bead cap onto a head pin. Make 16 components.

2 Follow steps 4-6 of "pearl cluster" with a 1-in. chain and eight components.

3 Attach the top-chain link on each cluster to the loop on an earring finding.

4 Make the second earring to match. •

– *Terri Torbeck*

materials

necklace
- **19** 7-7.5mm oblong pearls
- **19** 3mm flat daisy spacer beads
- **19** head pins, 1½ in. (4cm)
- **19** 6mm bead caps
- 1½ in. (4cm) chain with 2mm links
- 17 in. (44cm) satin cord, ⅛-in. (3mm) diameter, black
- 12 in. (30cm) 24-gauge twisted wire
- knitting needle, US size 8 (5mm)
- knitting needle, US size 3 (3.25mm)
- white glue

Optional: bail, 4 in. (10cm) 22-gauge twisted wire, 4 in. 22-gauge round wire

earrings
- **16** 3-4mm oblong pearls
- **16** head pins, 1½ in. (4cm)
- **16** size 15° seed beads, silver
- **16** 4mm bead caps
- 2 in. chain with 2mm links
- **2** earring wires

Tools: chainnose and roundnose pliers, diagonal wire cutters, small metal file

i

j

Braided
multi-strand collar